CO.

GW01398207

RECIPE

CREAM OF CRAB SOUP

All along the north Norfolk coast you will find a wonderful variety of excellent shellfish for sale, but the county is especially famous for its crabs. The small, fat crabs caught in Cromer Bay are reputedly the sweetest in the country, but excellent locally-caught crabs will be found for sale in many other places. Although crabs are available all year round, and are delicious eaten fresh as a dressed crab or in a crab salad, they are least expensive in the summer months, which is a good time to make this creamy soup, ideal for a dinner party or a special occasion.

You will need one large freshly cooked crab in its shell (or two smaller crabs) to produce about the weight of prepared crab meat needed for this recipe. If you are using a fresh crab in its shell, remove the meat as follows: lay the crab on its back, twist off the claws and legs and set aside. Push back the pointed flap curving under the body and press the body out of the shell. Remove and discard the greyish-white, feathery 'fingers', and the transparent stomach sac. Scoop out all the dark meat from the shell. Crack open the claws with a hammer or nutcracker and take out the light meat. Otherwise, you can buy fresh or frozen cooked crab meat from fishmongers or supermarkets in a mixture of dark and light meat. If you buy frozen crab meat, thaw it thoroughly before use.

25g/1oz butter
1 medium onion, peeled and finely chopped
1 celery stick, finely chopped
1 garlic clove, crushed
1½ tablespoonfuls plain flour
225g/8oz prepared weight of cooked crab meat,
   half dark and half light
1.2 litres/2 pints fish or chicken stock
150ml/ ¼ pint double cream
30ml/2 tablespoonfuls dry sherry
Salt and freshly ground black pepper

Flavours of...

NORFOLK

RECIPES

Compiled by Julia Skinner

THE FRANCIS FRITH COLLECTION

www.francisfrith.com

First published in the United Kingdom in 2011 by The Francis Frith Collection®

This edition published in 2014
ISBN 978-1-84589-840-3

British Library Cataloguing in Publication Data

Flavours of Norfolk - Recipes
Compiled by Julia Skinner

The Francis Frith Collection
6 Oakley Business Park,
Wylye Road, Dinton,
Wiltshire SP3 5EU
Tel: +44 (0) 1722 716 376
Email: info@francisfrith.co.uk
www.francisfrith.com

Printed and bound in England

Front Cover: **COLTISHALL, A CORNFIELD 1902** 48127p
Frontispiece: **HORNING, A WHERRY ON THE BROADS 1902** 48108

The colour-tinting is for illustrative purposes only, and is not intended to be historically accurate

Melt the butter in a large pan. Add the chopped onion, celery and garlic and cook over a medium heat for a few minutes, stirring frequently, until they are softened and transparent but not browned. Remove the pan from the heat and stir in the flour. Put the pan back on the heat and gradually add the stock, a little at a time and stirring continually. Bring the mixture to the boil, stirring constantly as it thickens, then reduce the heat, add the dark crab meat and simmer gently for about 30 minutes, stirring occasionally. Remove the pan from the heat and allow the soup to cool a little, then liquidise it in a blender or processor and return it to the cleaned out pan. Season to taste with salt and freshly ground black pepper. Chop the light crab meat into very small pieces and stir it into the soup, together with the sherry and the cream. Reheat the soup before serving, but do not allow it to boil.

CROMER, THE SANDS 1906 56855

SANDRINGHAM, THE HOUSE c1955 S58150

Norfolk's extensive arable fields of grain, coastal marshes and waterways of the Broads provide shelter for all kinds of game birds, such as partridge, pheasant, quail, woodcock and wild duck, and Norfolk is regarded as prime shooting country. Shooting parties have long been held on many of the county's country estates, including the royal estate of Sandringham, near King's Lynn, where the Royal Family traditionally gathers to celebrate the New Year. Sandringham has been a royal estate since the 1860s, when it was purchased for Queen Victoria's eldest son, the Prince of Wales, who reigned as Edward VII from 1901 to 1910. He was so fond of shooting at Sandringham that he ordered all the clocks on the estate to be set half an hour ahead of Greenwich Mean Time, to allow him extra time for his sport. The tradition of 'Sandringham Time' was kept on the estate from 1901 until 1936, when it was stopped by Edward VIII.

RECIPE

GAME SOUP

This soup makes good use of the carcasses and scraps of meat left after game birds such as pheasant, partridge or wild duck have been roasted and eaten.

> 1 onion
> 1 carrot
> 1 stick of celery
> 75g/3oz butter
> 1.2 litres/2 pints game stock, made from the carcasses
>   of 2 game birds
> Any meat picked from the carcasses, finely chopped
> 1 bay leaf
> Salt and pepper
> 25g/1oz plain flour
> 2 teaspoonfuls redcurrant jelly
> 2 tablespoonfuls sherry or red wine
> 2 teaspoonfuls lemon juice

Peel and chop the onion, scrub and chop the carrot, and wash and slice the celery. Melt 50g (2oz) of the butter in a large pan, and sauté the vegetables for 2-3 minutes, turning them over from time to time, until they are lightly browned. Add the stock, bay leaf, and salt and pepper to taste. Bring to the boil then reduce the heat, simmer gently for 1 hour, then strain and discard the vegetables and bay leaf. Melt the remaining butter in another pan, stir in the flour to make a roux and cook gently for 2-3 minutes, stirring. Gradually add the strained liquid to the roux, a little at a time, stirring continually so that no lumps are formed. Bring to the boil, then reduce the heat, add the finely chopped meat and simmer for 5 minutes. Just before serving, add the lemon juice, redcurrant jelly and sherry or wine. Reheat until the jelly has dissolved, then serve immediately.

KING'S LYNN, HIGH STREET
1908 60024

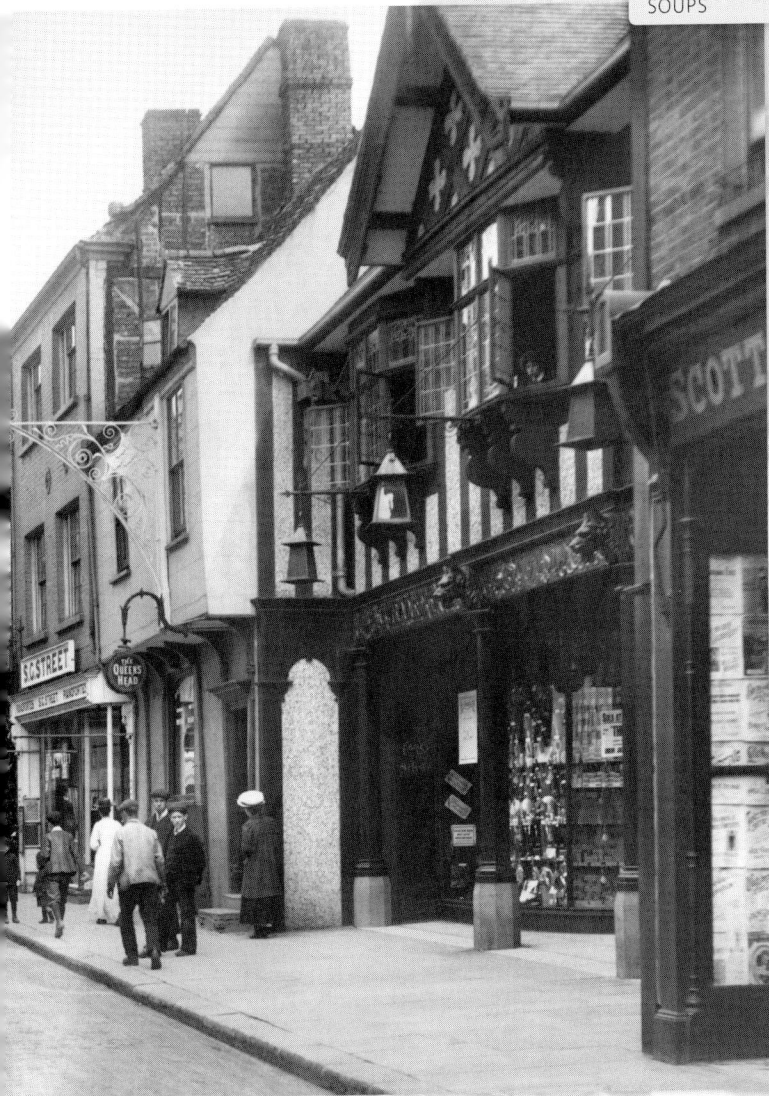

GREAT YARMOUTH FISH MARKET

Although the Norfolk port of Great Yarmouth was thriving in the Middle Ages, the town's prosperity was founded on herring fishing. The herring trade reached its height in the 19th century, when Great Yarmouth was the leading herring port in the world. During the main herring season, which lasted for about ten weeks from the end of September, the town's population would be swelled by thousands of fishermen with their wives and daughters, who gutted and packed the fish – this was a skilled job, and a good herring woman could gut 40 fish a minute. The photograph opposite shows the town's fish market around 1900. After a good fishing trip, the drifters have unloaded their haul into baskets known as 'swills', specially made wicker baskets for herrings that were unique to Great Yarmouth and Lowestoft in Suffolk. On the wharf the bowler-hatted tellers are assessing the catch prior to its sale by auction. Great Yarmouth's herring fishing industry continued up to the second half of the 20th century, but by the 1950s it was clear that fish stocks were depleted, and the herring industry eventually came to an end. Great Yarmouth's once-mighty herring fleet is now gone, but the town's fishing heritage is commemorated in the excellent Time and Tide museum on Blackfriar's Road, housed in a former herring smokery.

From the Middle Ages onwards there were many smokehouses in Great Yarmouth where herrings were turned into 'red herrings' (salted herrings that were smoked for up to 6 weeks until they were hard and dry – originally to ensure a long preservation in medieval times), kippers, buckling (herring hot-smoked with the guts and roe left in) and the famous Yarmouth bloaters for which the town was renowned. A bloater is a whole ungutted

GREAT YARMOUTH, THE FISH MARKET c1900 G56503

herring that is not split open down the back, like a kipper, before being lightly smoked for up to 12 hours – they are delicious, with a slightly gamey flavour. They should be eaten straight after coming from the smoker, and certainly within 48 hours, and are best served either as they are bought fresh, without further cooking, or simply grilled with butter and eaten with bread and butter; cooked bloaters are also good made into bloater paste, by removing the flesh from the bones and pounding it with half its weight of butter and a little lemon juice and pepper to make a savoury spread. These traditional products are still made in Great Yarmouth by HS Fishing 2000 Ltd at the Smoke House at Sutton Road, South Denes, although most of the herring and mackerel that are smoked there come from Norway nowadays.

GREAT YARMOUTH, KING STREET 1896 37958

RECIPE

HERRINGS WITH MUSTARD SAUCE

This recipe recalls the importance of herrings to Great Yarmouth in the past, with herrings filled with a savoury stuffing and served with a mustard sauce for a tasty lunch or supper for 4 people. Mustard sauce is a traditional accompaniment to herrings in many parts of Britain, including Norfolk, which has an important mustard industry. Bright yellow fields of mustard have been grown in Norfolk ever since Jeremiah Colman took over Stoke Holy Cross Mill near Norwich in 1814 and started milling mustard seed, making his fiery condiment from a closely guarded formula of ground and blended brown and white mustard seeds. In 1823 Jeremiah went into partnership with his adopted nephew James, as J & J Colman, and in 1973 the Colman company celebrated 150 years of business by opening The Mustard Shop in the Royal Arcade in Norwich. Now run by HEART, the city's Heritage, Economic and Regeneration Trust, Colman's Mustard Shop and Museum is one of Norwich's popular tourist attractions.

4 large herrings
3 heaped tablespoonfuls fresh white breadcrumbs
1 heaped teaspoonful finely chopped parsley
A squeeze of lemon juice
Grated rind of half a lemon
Salt and black pepper
Oil for frying
25g/1oz butter
Lemon wedges and fresh parsley sprigs for garnish

For the mustard sauce
40g/1½ oz butter
25g/1oz plain flour
450ml/ ¾ pint milk
Salt and black pepper
1 level tablespoonful dry mustard powder
1 tablespoonful wine vinegar
1 level teaspoonful caster sugar

Pre-heat the oven to 200°C/400°F/Gas Mark 6.

Remove the heads from the herrings, clean, gut and bone them, then wash the fish and pat them thoroughly dry. Put the breadcrumbs, parsley, lemon juice and lemon rind in a basin, and season lightly with salt and freshly ground black pepper. Melt the butter and stir it into the breadcrumbs to bind the mixture, which should now be moist, but crumbly.

Stuff the herrings with the breadcrumb mixture, and if necessary secure them with wooden cocktail sticks. Slash the skins crossways two or three times on each side; brush the herrings with oil and wrap each fish separately in foil. Put the herrings in a well-buttered deep ovenproof dish; cover with lightly buttered greaseproof paper and bake in the centre of the pre-heated oven at for 35-40 minutes. Just before the herrings are cooked, make the mustard sauce as directed below.

To make the mustard sauce: melt 25g/1oz of the butter in a pan; stir in the flour and cook for 1 minute. Gradually stir in the milk, a little at a time and stirring continually until the sauce has thickened and is quite smooth. Bring to the boil, then reduce the heat and simmer for 2-3 minutes, stirring; season to taste with salt and pepper. Blend the mustard powder with the vinegar and stir it into the sauce, and add the sugar. Check the seasoning again, then stir in the remaining butter until it has melted.

Transfer the baked herrings to a hot serving dish and garnish with wedges of lemon and sprigs of parsley. Serve, with the mustard sauce handed round separately.

GORLESTON, THE HARBOUR 1894 33393

RECIPE

SOUSED HERRINGS

This was a popular way of preparing fresh herrings in East Anglia in the past, allowing a glut of herrings to be cooked and preserved. It makes an ideal lunch or supper dish, and once the herrings have been 'soused', they can be kept in the fridge for several days if necessary. Fresh mackerel can also be prepared the same way.

> 4 herrings, filleted
> 25g/1oz plain flour
> Half a teaspoonful of powdered mace
> 25g/1oz butter
> Salt and pepper
> 1 teaspoonful of chopped fresh parsley
> 1 bay leaf
> 150ml/ ¼ pint water
> 150ml/ ¼ pint malt vinegar

Pre-heat the oven to 190°C/375°F/Gas Mark 5.

Mix the flour with the salt, pepper and mace, and use it to dust the herring fillets. Place a small knob of butter in the centre of each fillet, sprinkle the fillet with chopped parsley and roll it up, skin side out. Secure each herring roll with a wooden cocktail stick.

Place the herrings in an ovenproof dish, and add the water, vinegar and bay leaf. Cover the dish and bake for 1 hour in the pre-heated oven. Remove from the oven and leave the herrings to cool completely in the cooking liquid before serving. Eat cold, serve with slices of bread and butter.

RECIPES

NORFOLK FISH PIE

The sea fishing industry that was once so important to Norfolk's economy has declined dramatically in recent decades. However, a little offshore fishing continues, with catches such as cod, skate, sea bass, mackerel, ling and whiting. This traditional Norfolk recipe for a fish pie includes cider, for which the county is also famous. Cider made in Norfolk, such as that made by the award-winning Norfolk Cider Company, uses juice from cooking or dessert apple varieties and so has a less astringent character than the cider made elsewhere in England, which uses juice from sharp cider apples.

> 450g/1 lb cod fillet, skinned and cut into small cubes
> 300ml/ ½ pint cider
> 450g/1 lb potatoes
> Salt and pepper
> A little milk for mashing the potatoes
> 25g/1oz butter or margarine
> 25g/1oz plain flour
> 2 tomatoes, sliced
> 50g/2oz grated tasty cheese of choice

Peel the potatoes and boil them in lightly salted water until they are cooked, then mash with a little milk and keep warm. Whilst they are cooking, put the cod pieces in a saucepan with the cider, bring to the boil, then reduce the heat, cover the pan and simmer until the fish is cooked and will flake easily. Drain the fish – reserving the cider that it was cooked in – and keep warm. Melt the butter or margarine in a saucepan, then stir in the flour. Cook, stirring, for two minutes, then gradually add the reserved cider, stirring all the time. Bring to the boil, stirring continually, until the sauce has thickened and is smooth. Season to taste with salt and pepper. Spoon the mashed potato around the edge of a flameproof serving dish, and put the cooked fish in the centre. Pour the sauce over the fish, arrange the tomato slices on top and sprinkle with the grated cheese. Either brown in a pre-heated oven at 190°C/375°F/Gas Mark 5 for 15 minutes, or under a pre-heated hot grill.

SKATE WINGS WITH LEMON AND CAPER BUTTER

A fish caught off the Norfolk coast is the flat ray-shaped skate. The soft flesh of skate wings has a delicate flavour, and is easily picked off the bony wings after cooking. Ask your fishmonger to skin the wings for you if possible – if not, it is easier to remove the skin after the wings have been cooked, before serving them. This zesty dressing is also good with plaice and Dover or lemon sole. Serves 4.

2 skate wings, each weighing about 550g (1¼ lbs)
Half a lemon, cut into thin slices
1 small onion, peeled and cut into thin slices
1 small bay leaf
2-3 peppercorns
3-4 stalks of parsley
½ level teaspoonful salt
For the dressing:
Juice of 2 lemons
50g/2oz unsalted butter
4 teaspoonfuls capers, drained and rinsed
1 tablespoonful chopped fresh parsley

Rinse the skate, wipe it dry then cut each wing in half, to make four portions. Place in a saucepan large enough to hold the wings in a single layer. Pour in 300ml (½ pint) of boiling water, and add the sliced lemon and onion, bay leaf, peppercorns, parsley stalks and salt. Bring the water back to the boil, then reduce the heat, cover the pan and simmer gently for 10-15 minutes, until the flesh is tender and parts easily from the bone. Remove the fish from the pan with a slotted spoon and drain well. (Peel off the skin now, if necessary.) Arrange the fish on a hot serving dish, and keep warm whilst you make the dressing. Add 4 tablespoonfuls of water to the lemon juice. Heat the butter in a heavy-based pan until it is melted and browned, but not scorched. Add the lemon juice, half at first, then taste the sauce and add the other half if you want. Add the capers and parsley, and season well to taste. Pour the dressing over the fish and serve, with vegetables such as new potatoes and peas, green beans or wilted spinach.

SHERINGHAM, FISHERMEN MENDING CRAB POTS 1906 56879

Norfolk's sea-fishing industry is now just a shadow of its former glory, but the shellfish industry is thriving all along the county's long northern coastline, where high-quality crabs, oysters, mussels, cockles, whelks, shrimps and lobster are caught or farmed in many places. The small village of Stiffkey (pronounced 'Stookey') between Blakeney and Wells-next-the-Sea is famous for the blue-shelled cockles known as 'Stookey (or Stewkey) Blues' that are found there, Cromer is renowned for its crabs and Wells-next-the-Sea for the quality of its locally-caught whelks. Several shrimping vessels operate out of King's Lynn and bring in their catch to be sold in the town. Norfolk also has a significant oyster industry, with particular centres at Thornham and Brancaster Staithe, where Pacific oysters, also known as 'Gigas', are farmed, as well as excellent mussels. The recipe on the opposite page is a favourite Norfolk way of eating cockles.

RECIPE

COCKLES AND BACON

600ml/1 pint (volume) fresh cockles
A little oil or lard for frying
8 rashers of streaky bacon
Bread slices for toast
Butter

Wash the cockles thoroughly in plenty of cold water, or leave them to soak for several hours if possible. Bring a large saucepan of water to the boil. Place the cockles in the water and leave for a few minutes, until their shells have opened. Remove from heat, strain and leave the cockles to cool. When they have cooled, pick the cockles out of their shells. Fry the bacon rashers in a little oil or lard until they are crisp, then remove from the pan and keep warm. Add the cockles to the pan and toss them in the bacon fat until they are lightly browned. Serve the cockles and bacon on slices of hot buttered toast.

WELLS-NEXT-THE-SEA, WHELK BOATS AT THE QUAY
1929 81998

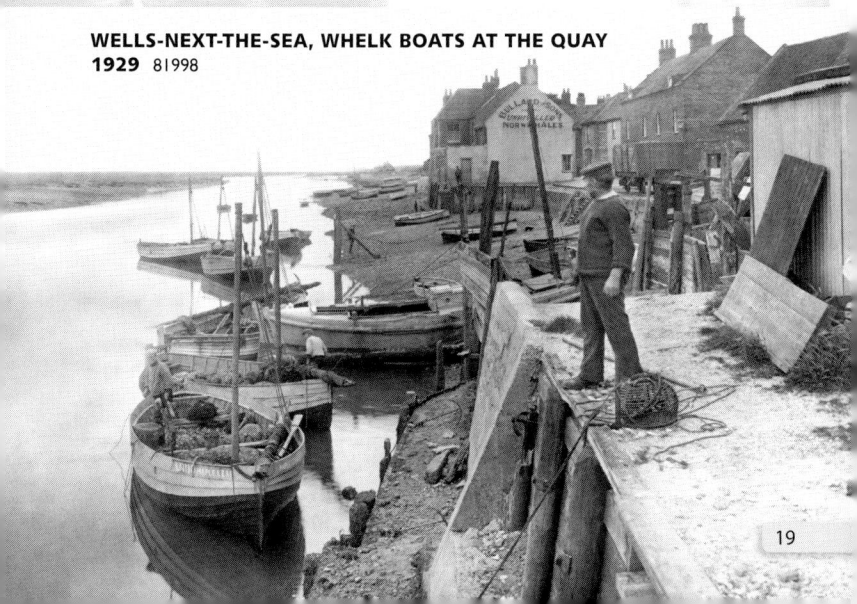

RECIPE

The recipe on the opposite page for Norfolk Lamb Parcels comes from north Norfolk, an area famous for the quality and flavour of the lamb reared there. A boned breast of lamb is relatively cheap, and makes an economical meal. It is best cooked slowly, so that the fat bastes the meat in the roasting tin. It is usually prepared with the meat kept in one piece, spread with a savoury stuffing and then rolled up like a Swiss roll and tied with string, but in this recipe the meat is cut into portions, and then layered like a sandwich with the stuffing, and tied up into individual 'parcels'.

EAST BARSHAM, SHEEP ON THE FAKENHAM ROAD 1929 82041

NORFOLK LAMB PARCELS

The quantities in this recipe are for a small breast of lamb weighing about 625g (1½ lbs), which will make 2 parcels to feed 2-4 people, depending on appetite. Adjust the quantities to feed more people, or using a larger piece of meat.

1 boned breast of lamb, about 625g/1½ lbs in weight
2 tablespoonfuls olive oil
25g/1oz butter
Salt and pepper
1 onion, peeled and finely chopped
150ml/ ¼ pint chicken or vegetable stock
50g/2oz fresh breadcrumbs
115g/4oz sausagemeat
   (open some sausages if you can't get sausagemeat)
1 dessertspoonful finely chopped fresh sage leaves
1 dessertspoonful chutney, any flavour of choice

Pre-heat the oven to 200°C/400°F/Gas Mark 6.

To make the stuffing, heat 1 tablespoonful of the oil in a large saucepan, add the chopped onion and cook gently until it is soft and transparent, but not browned. Add the stock, bring to the boil and boil for about 5 minutes, until the liquid is well reduced down. Remove the pan from the heat and add the breadcrumbs, sausagemeat, chopped sage and chutney. Season to taste and blend it all together to make a thick paste. Leave to cool and firm up for about 5 minutes. Cut the breast of lamb into 4 equal pieces, then spread the stuffing mixture over two of the pieces. Put the other two pieces of meat on top, to form two 'sandwiches', then tie each 'sandwich' up like a parcel with kitchen string, securing all four sides. Put the parcels in a roasting tin and season with salt and pepper. Melt the remaining oil and butter together in a pan, then brush it over the tops and sides of the parcels. Cover the tin with foil and put in the pre-heated oven. Roast the meat for 30 minutes, then reduce the oven temperature to 180°C/350°F/Gas Mark 4 and roast for a further 1½ hours, basting the meat every half hour. At the end of this time, remove the tin foil and roast for another 15 minutes before serving.

RECIPE

NORFOLK PLOUGH PUDDING

It used to be the custom for this pudding to be served on Plough Monday, the first Monday after Twelfth Night (January 5th). Plough Monday marked the end of the Christmas holiday period for farm labourers, and was traditionally the date for spring ploughing to begin.

225g/8oz self-raising flour
115g/4oz shredded suet
450g/1 lb pork sausage meat
115g/4oz streaky bacon, de-rinded and chopped into small pieces
1 onion, peeled and finely chopped
1 dessertspoonful of chopped fresh sage
   (or a teaspoonful of chopped dried sage)
1 teaspoonful brown sugar
Salt and pepper

Grease a 1.2 litre (2 pint) pudding bowl. Mix together the flour and suet, a pinch of salt, and enough cold water to bind it all together into a firm dough. Roll out the dough on a floured surface and use two-thirds of it to line the pudding bowl. Mix together the sausage meat, chopped bacon, onion, sage and sugar, and season with salt and pepper. Press the meat mixture into the pudding bowl, and use the remaining pastry to make a lid, sealing the edges together well. Cover the pudding bowl with a lid of pleated greaseproof paper and a further piece of pleated foil (to allow room for expansion during cooking), and tie down well. Place the pudding bowl in a large saucepan and pour in enough boiling water to come half way up the bowl. Cover the pan with its lid, bring the water back to the boil and steam the pudding over boiling water for 4 hours, topping up the saucepan with more boiling water from time to time to ensure that the pan does not boil dry. When cooked, turn out the pudding onto a warm serving dish and serve piping hot, with a thick brown gravy or tomato sauce.

COLTISHALL, IN A CORNFIELD 1902 48127x

RECIPE

HONEY ROASTED TURKEY
WITH CANDIED POTATOES

For centuries Norfolk has been renowned for the quality of the turkeys reared in the county. In the 17th century flocks of the famous Norfolk Black turkeys were driven on foot from Norfolk to London for the Christmas markets, in great droves of 500 birds or more. The journey took about 3 months, and the birds had their feet coated in tar to protect them on the journey. This Norfolk recipe for cooking turkey also produces delicious potatoes, candied from the honey in the pan. The gravy to accompany the turkey should be made separately, as the honey in the pan will make it too sweet if the cooking juices are used in the usual way. Allow a total cooking time of 15 minutes roasting per 450g (1 lb) weight of the turkey.

>   1 turkey, between 3.5-5.5kg (8-12 lbs) in weight
>   225g/8oz honey
>   115g/4oz butter
>   1.4kg/3 lb potatoes, peeled and halved

Gently melt the honey and butter together in a pan and stir well to mix it. Place the turkey in a roasting tin and pour the honey and butter mixture all over it. Leave the turkey to stand for an hour, basting occasionally with the mixture that has run off into the tray. Pre-heat the oven to 200°C/400°F/Gas Mark 6. Arrange the potatoes around the turkey, place the roasting tin in the pre-heated oven and cook for 40 minutes. The honey will make a dark crust over the bird, sealing in the flavour. After 40 minutes, baste the turkey with the mixture that has run off into the tin and turn the potatoes, reduce the oven heat to 180°C/350°F/Gas Mark 4 and cook for a further 30 minutes. Baste the turkey and turn the potatoes again, then cover the roasting tin with foil and continue to cook in accordance with the time scale above. Remove the foil for the last 15 minutes of cooking time to allow the skin to crisp.

RECIPE

ROAST WILD DUCK

The Broads area of Norfolk is particularly known for the variety of wildfowl to be found there. Both wild duck and geese formed an important part of the local diet in past times. Wild duck, such as mallard, teal and widgeon, should not be overcooked – allow a roasting time of between 30-50 minutes, depending on the size of the bird.

> 1 wild duck
> A knob of butter
> Orange juice
>
> For the sauce:
> 1 tablespoonful of lemon juice
> 1 tablespoonful of sugar
> 2 tablespoonfuls of port wine
> 1 tablespoonful of tomato ketchup
> Salt
> Cayenne pepper

Pre-heat the oven to 190°C/375°F/Gas Mark 5.

Put the duck in a roasting tin. Place a knob of butter inside the duck, and pour some orange juice over the bird. Roast in the pre-heated oven for about 30-50 minutes (depending on the size of the bird) until it is tender, basting occasionally with the juices in the tin. When the duck is cooked, remove it from the roasting tin and keep it warm whilst you make the sauce. Add the sauce ingredients to the juices in the roasting tin, then bring to the boil, stirring well. Serve the duck, with the sauce handed round separately.

RECIPE

AUTUMN RABBIT AND NORFOLK DUMPLINGS

In previous centuries Norfolk was overrun with rabbits. When farm workers 'lived in' on the farms, rabbits formed a large part of their diet and were known as 'hollow meat'. In fact, some farmworkers got so bored of eating rabbit that a proviso had to be made that they should only be fed 'hollow meat' for a certain number of days a week.

> 1 rabbit, jointed
> 25g/1oz lard
> 25g/1oz plain flour
> 300ml/ ½ pint ale or beer
> 1 onion
> 1 carrot
> 1 large cooking apple
> 50g/2oz button mushrooms
> A sprig each of fresh parsley and thyme
> 1 bay leaf
> Salt and pepper

Oven temperature: 180°C/350°F/Gas Mark 4.

Melt the lard in a large heavy pan, add the rabbit joints and brown them. Remove the rabbit from the pan and place in a casserole dish. Stir the flour into the hot fat in the pan, cook for a few minutes, then add the ale or beer a little at a time, stirring continuously until the sauce thickens. Pour the sauce over the rabbit joints in the casserole. Peel and slice the onion, carrot and apple, and add to the casserole. Chop the mushrooms and herbs and add to the casserole, together with the bay leaf. Season with salt and pepper. Cover the casserole dish with its lid, and cook in a moderate oven for about 2 hours, until the rabbit is tender. Remove the bay leaf before serving.

Put the Norfolk Dumplings (see recipe on opposite page) on top of the casserole for the last 25-30 minutes of the cooking time.

NORFOLK DUMPLINGS

In Norfolk, dumplings cooked on top of a stew are called 'floaters' or 'swimmers'. They are light, and do not contain suet (heavy suet dumplings are known disparagingly in Norfolk as 'sinkers'). There is some argument as to whether Norfolk dumplings should contain yeast or not – although there is a version made with yeast, like a bread dough, a recipe for the non-yeast version is given here.

Allow 1 heaped tablespoonful of self-raising flour per person (or use plain flour and 1 teaspoonful of baking powder), a pinch of salt and water to mix. Sieve the flour and salt into a bowl. Add sufficient water to make a light dough. Turn out onto a floured surface, knead lightly, then divide into the required amount of pieces and form into round dumplings. Place them on top of the casserole for the last 25-30 minutes of cooking time.

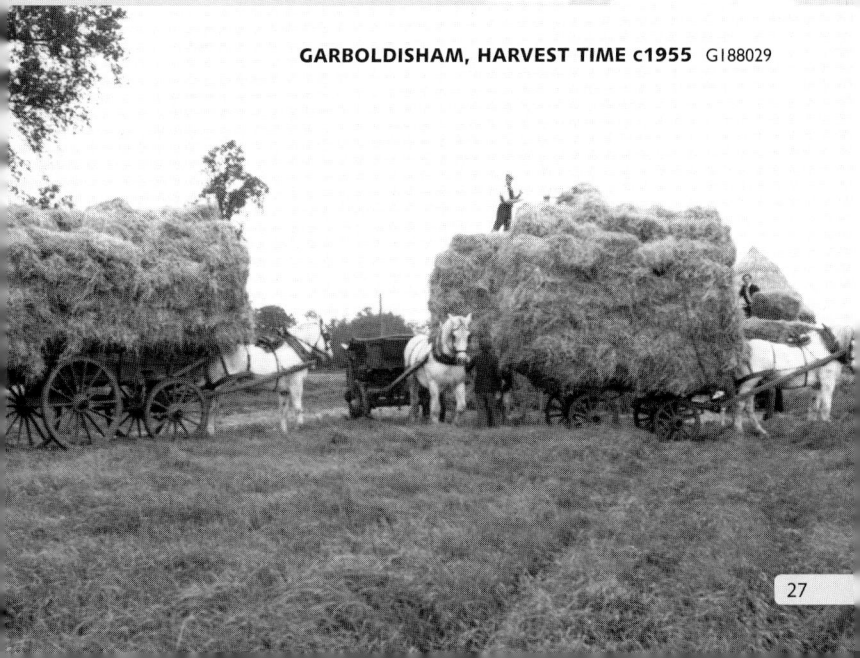

GARBOLDISHAM, HARVEST TIME c1955 GI88029

RECIPE

OVEN-BAKED CARROTS WITH HONEY AND MUSTARD

Norfolk boasts some of the most fertile soil in the UK, and is an important region for the production of vegetables. Major crops are cabbage, peas, leeks, brussels sprouts and potatoes, but the county is particularly famous for its root vegetables, parsnips, swede, turnips and carrots. Norfolk is one of the UK's main carrot growing areas. This is an unusual way of cooking carrots to serve as a vegetable accompaniment, which gives them a wonderful flavour.

> 450g/1 lb carrots
> 2 tablespoonfuls of water
> 2 tablespoonfuls of sunflower oil
> 2 tablespoonfuls of runny honey
> 1 tablespoonful of whole-grain mustard
> Salt and freshly ground black pepper

Pre-heat the oven to 190°C/375°F/Gas Mark 5.

Scrub the carrots and trim off the ends, then chop them into chunky sticks. Put the carrot pieces into a shallow ovenproof dish.

In a bowl, mix together the water, oil, honey and mustard, and season to taste with a little salt and freshly ground black pepper. Pour the mixture over the carrots in the oven dish, and stir until the carrots have all been coated with the mixture.

Cover the dish with its lid, or a piece of close-fitting kitchen foil, and bake in the pre-heated oven for 50-60 minutes, until the carrots are tender.

HORNING 1902   48107

RECIPE

BUTTERED TURNIPS IN CREAM AND PARSLEY SAUCE

Norfolk has been associated with the turnip since the 1730s when Charles, 2nd Viscount Townshend popularised the large-scale cultivation of turnips as winter fodder for animals from his Norfolk estate at Raynham Hall, near Fakenham. His enthusiastic promotion of turnips earned him the nickname of 'Turnip Townshend', but he is now recognised as one of the key names in the agricultural revolution of the 18th century. Turnips have been a popular vegetable for human consumption for centuries. The larger varieties of turnip, like Norfolk Purple Top, are usually eaten boiled and mashed, but a number of varieties have been developed which are harvested when they are small, young and tender, about the size of a golf ball, and cooked whole. This is a delicious way of serving small turnips – the cream sauce really brings out their delicate, slightly peppery flavour. Serves 3-4.

> 450g/1 lb very small young turnips, topped, tailed and peeled, but left whole (if larger turnips are used, up to the size of a cricket ball, peel them and cut them into quarters)
> 25g/1oz butter
> 150ml/5 fl oz/¼ pint chicken stock
> 1 teaspoonful sugar
> Salt and freshly ground black pepper
> 1 tablespoonful finely chopped fresh parsley
> 150ml/5 fl oz/¼ pint double cream, the thickest you can get

Melt the butter over a medium heat in a large saucepan. Add the peeled turnips, turn to coat them all over with the melted butter, and cook gently for about 10 minutes, shaking them frequently, so that they fry to a light golden colour all over. Pour in the stock, add the sugar and season to taste. Bring to the boil, then reduce the heat to simmering point, cover the pan and cook the turnips for 20 minutes, shaking the pan now and then so they don't stick. Remove the cooked turnips to a warm serving dish and keep hot. Stir the cream into the liquid remaining in the pan, add the parsley and warm through. Check for seasoning, then pour the sauce over the turnips in the dish and serve.

**NORTH WALSHAM
MARKET PLACE
1921** 70934

ARTISAN CHEESEMAKERS

A number of artisan cheesemakers are producing some excellent local cheeses in Norfolk nowadays. Here are a few to look out for:

Fine cheeses are produced by Ferndale Norfolk Farmhouse Cheeses at Little Barningham, ten miles south-west of Cromer. Amongst their range is Norfolk Dapple, an award-winning cheddar-type hard cheese with a full flavour, which develops a distinctive dappled rind as it ripens; Ruby Dapple, a cheddar-type full-flavoured cheese made with the addition of port, which also develops a distinctive dappled rind as it ripens; and Norfolk Carrow, another hard cheddar-type cheese with a dappled rind, which is made with the addition of mustard seeds. Another interesting cheese made by the company is Norfolk Tawny, which has a rind that is washed four times during the cheese-making process with 'Men of Norfolk' dark ale.

Binham Blue is a wonderful creamy, tangy blue cheese, rather like Gorgonzola, that is made by Mrs Temple's Cheeses at Copys Green Farm, Wighton, near Wells-next-the-Sea in north Norfolk. Mrs Temple's Cheeses also makes a wide range of other great cheeses, including the crumbly-textured Walsingham, Wells Alpine (also known as Norfolk Alpine), a semi-hard cheese with a characteristic flavour which is made from the milk of Brown Swiss cows, and Wighton Cheese, a soft cheese that is made in wicker moulds, which gives its exterior an attractive basketwork pattern.

An unusual cheese is the delightfully-named Norfolk White Lady, which is made from full-fat unpasteurised sheeps' milk by Willow Farm Dairy at Deopham, near Wymondham. This brie-style cheese is made with vegetarian rennet, using the milk from a herd of British Friesland dairy ewes. It has a wonderful creamy texture, and a flavour that improves with age. Willow Farm Dairy also makes Wissington Cheese from ewes' milk, a hard cheese that is full of flavour, which has been compared to Manchego.

THE BROADS, HOME AT
EVENING c1900   T213078

ASPARAGUS

Asparagus is cultivated on a large scale in many parts of East Anglia, including Norfolk. This great English delicacy is only available for a short season, from May to early July. Asparagus should be cooked and eaten as soon as possible after being picked, preferably on the same day, for its flavour to be enjoyed at its best. The recipe on the opposite page uses asparagus and Norfolk's Binham Blue Cheese from Mrs Temple's Cheeses (see page 32) to make a savoury flan, ideal for a summer lunch or picnic. If you can't get Binham Blue, use another creamy blue cheese such as Saint Agur, Gorgonzola or Cambozola, which are easily available in supermarkets. To prepare the fresh asparagus spears, trim off any woody ends and lightly scrape off any scales from the lowest parts of the stems, scraping away from the delicate tips.

POOR MAN'S ASPARAGUS

Asparagus is widely cultivated in Norfolk, but a wild plant rather like it is also popular. Marsh Samphire, or glasswort, grows on salt marshes around the Norfolk coast, and is gathered for sale commercially when in season. The green fleshy tips of samphire should be washed and trimmed of any coarse roots, then steamed or cooked in boiling water for 6-8 minutes, until tender but still with some 'bite' to it. Samphire can either be served hot, with melted butter, or cold in a salad, with a vinaigrette dressing. It also goes very well with lamb, fish and shellfish. Samphire is often known as 'poor man's asparagus', but it is also enjoyed by the rich – it was served at the royal wedding breakfast of Prince Charles and Lady Diana Spencer in 1981, as a symbol of Sandringham in Norfolk, where the royal family has a residence.

RECIPE

ASPARAGUS AND BINHAM BLUE CHEESE FLAN

225g/8oz plain flour
115g/4oz butter or margarine
Salt and freshly ground black pepper
115g/4oz asparagus spears, prepared weight (see opposite)
3 eggs, plus 1 egg yolk
150ml/ ¼ pint double cream
115g/4oz Binham Blue Cheese, or alternative (see opposite)

Pre-heat the oven to 200°F/400°F/Gas Mark 6 and place a baking tray in the oven to heat up. Grease a flan dish or tin about 20-22cms (8-9 inches) in diameter. Sift the flour into a mixing bowl with a pinch of salt, and rub in the butter or margarine. Add just enough cold water to mix it into a firm dough, and knead lightly until it is smooth and elastic. Roll out the dough and use it to line the flan dish. Prick the base with a fork all over to allow any air bubbles to escape during cooking, and place a piece of greaseproof paper with some baking beans on the pastry base. Place the dish on the baking tray in the pre-heated oven and bake blind for 10 minutes until the pastry is set, then remove the beans and paper and cook for a further 5 minutes to dry out the base. Remove from the oven, and reduce the oven temperature to 180°C/350°F/Gas Mark 4.

Blanch the prepared asparagus in lightly salted, rapidly boiling water for 2-3 minutes until it is just tender. Drain, then refresh it by rinsing it under cold running water, then drain well. Arrange pieces of blue cheese in the pastry case, then arrange the asparagus on top. Use a balloon whisk to mix the eggs, egg yolk and cream together, season well with salt and freshly ground black pepper, and pour the mixture into the pastry case over the cheese and asparagus. Stand the dish on the baking tray in the oven and bake at the reduced temperature for 15-20 minutes, or until the filling is just set and firm in the centre. Remove from the oven and leave to settle in the tin for at least 15 minutes before cutting and serving. This can be eaten warm or cold.

RECIPE

NORFOLK MILLION PIE

Puddings, pies and tarts were often made with sweet root vegetables in the past, such as carrots, pumpkins, marrows and parsnips. 'Million' was the old name for any sort of gourd, such as melon, pumpkin or marrow, and this traditional pie from Norfolk was originally made with pumpkin. The recipe was carried to the New World by the Pilgrim Fathers in the 17th century, many of whom came from East Anglia, and is recalled in the American tradition of eating Pumpkin Pie at Thanksgiving dinners, when the Pilgrim Fathers are commemorated. In Norfolk, it became more common in later centuries to make Million Pie with marrow. Nowadays, either marrow or pumpkin can be used in this recipe for a sweet dessert pie, as you prefer.

> 225g/8oz shortcrust pastry
> 450/1 lb pumpkin or vegetable marrow, with the peel, pith
> and seeds removed, cut into slices about 2.5cm (1 inch) thick
> 300ml/ ½ pint water
> 50g/2oz apricot or greengage jam
> 1½ tablespoonfuls soft brown sugar
> 1 egg, beaten
> Grated rind of half a lemon
> 1 teaspoonful lemon juice
> 1 teaspoonful ground nutmeg
> 25g/1oz currants or raisins

Bring the water to the boil in a large pan, add the pumpkin or marrow pieces, and boil for about 10 minutes, stirring occasionally to prevent sticking, until they are soft. Drain very well, then leave to cool. Pre-heat the oven to 200°C/400°F/Gas Mark 6. Roll out the pastry and use it to line a greased 20-22cm (8-9 inch) flan dish or pie tin. Trim the edges and keep the pastry trimmings. Spread the jam over the pastry base.

Add the egg, lemon rind and juice and most of the nutmeg and sugar to the cooled pumpkin or marrow, and beat it all together well with a fork until it is well mixed and smooth (or put the mixture through a blender if preferred). Mix in the currants or raisins, then turn the mixture into the pie case, and spread it evenly on top of the jam. Sprinkle the top with the reserved nutmeg and sugar. Roll out the pastry trimmings and cut them into thin strips, then make a lattice pattern with them across the top of the flan, twisting them to look pretty. Crimp all round the flan by pressing down with the end of a fork and your thumb so that you get a pattern around the pastry edge, and the strips are firmly stuck down. Bake in the pre-heated oven for 15 minutes, then reduce the oven temperature to 180°C/350°F/Gas Mark 4 and cook for a further 15-20 minutes, until the pastry is golden brown. This can be eaten hot or cold, served with cream.

DOWNHAM MARKET, THE CLOCK TOWER 1952 D149009

RECIPE

NORFOLK TREACLE CUSTARD TART

This is one of the recipes for which Norfolk is famous. It is an unusual treacle tart because it does not contain breadcrumbs. Instead, eggs and cream are used to form a delicious thick, sweet, buttery baked-custard-style filling.

For the pastry:
175g/6oz plain flour
Pinch of salt
75g/3oz butter or margarine

For the filling:
115g/4oz unsalted butter
8 tablespoonfuls golden syrup
Finely grated zest of 2 lemons
4 tablespoonfuls double cream
2 eggs, beaten

First, make the pastry. Sift the flour and salt into a mixing bowl, and rub in the butter or margarine until the mixture resembles fine breadcrumbs. Use a round-bladed knife to stir in 2-3 tablespoonfuls of cold water, until the mixture can be gathered into a ball of dough. Knead the dough lightly until it is smooth and elastic, then put it into the fridge to rest for 30 minutes, wrapped in clingfilm or in a plastic bag.

Pre-heat the oven to 190°C/375°F/Gas Mark 5 (slightly less for a fan oven), and place a baking tray in the oven to heat up. Grease a 20-22cm (8-9 inch) round tart tin. Roll out the pastry and use it to line the tin, and prick the base all over with a fork to allow air bubbles to escape during cooking. Gently warm the butter and syrup together in a pan – just enough for the butter to melt and dissolve. Remove the pan from the heat and allow the mixture to cool a little. Beat the eggs and cream together in a large bowl. Add the lemon zest, then gradually beat in the butter and syrup mixture. Pour the mixture into the pastry case. Put the tart in the centre of the pre-heated oven and bake for 25-30 minutes, until the pastry is crisp and golden and the filling is bubbling and starting to set. Remove from the oven and allow it to cool, when the filling will thicken and set firm. This can be eaten warm or cold.

KING'S LYNN, CHILDREN IN HIGH STREET
1908 60023x

RECIPE

CHARTER PUDDINGS

From 1773 until his death in 1803, Reverend James Woodforde lived at Weston Longville near Norwich, which he described as 'the fairest City in England'. Reverend Woodforde is famous for his diaries, published as 'The Diary of a Country Parson', which are a fascinating record of life in 18th-century rural England. In 1777 he recorded that he ate a 'Charter' at the home of a neighbouring cleric, which is believed to be this dish. This recipe makes 6 individual Charter Puddings.

> 570ml/1 pint single cream
> Grated rind of 1 lemon
> 2 eggs
> 2 egg yolks
> 50g/2oz caster sugar
> 12 fresh apricots, halved and stoned (or dried apricots,
> soaked overnight and poached in water until tender)

Put the cream in a bowl and stir in the lemon rind. Cover with cling film and leave in the fridge for at least one hour (preferably overnight), for the flavour to infuse. Pre-heat the oven to 150°C/300°F/Gas Mark 2, and grease 6 ramekin dishes. Beat together the eggs and egg yolks in a bowl with a fork or balloon whisk, pour in the steeped cream through a sieve, and stir in the sugar. Beat it all together, then pour the mixture into the dishes. Stand the dishes in a deep roasting tray, and pour in enough boiling water to come halfway up their sides. Cover the tray with foil, and bake in the centre of the pre-heated oven for 30-35 minutes, then check one of the puddings with a sharp knife – if the knife comes out just slightly creamy they are done, as they will continue to cook as they cool. If they seem far too runny, take off the foil and bake for another 10 minutes. Take the tray out of the oven, remove the dishes from the water and leave the puddings to cool, when they will thicken and firm up completely. Cut the apricots into thin slices, and arrange them over the top of the puddings before serving. Charter Puddings can be served either warm or cold.

NORWICH, DAVEY PLACE 1922 72602

NORWICH, MARKET PLACE 1929 81796

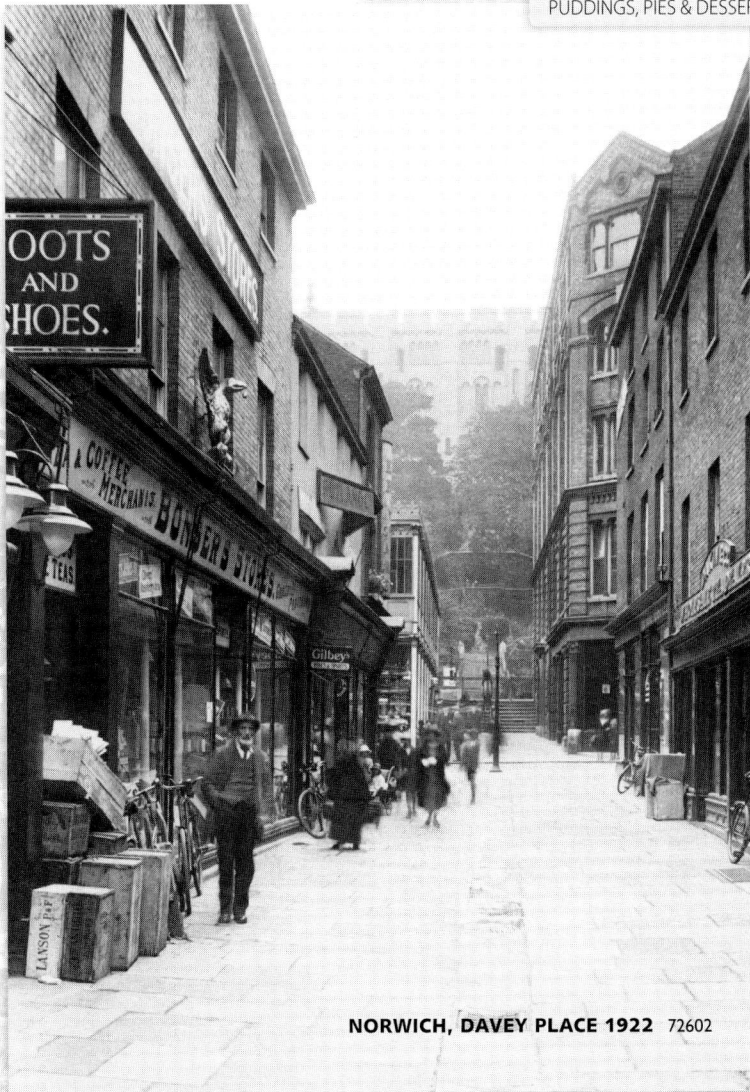

NORWICH, DAVEY PLACE 1922 72602

NORWICH, MARKET PLACE 1929 81796

RECIPES

NORWICH TART

<u>For the pastry:</u>
175g/6oz plain flour
Pinch of salt
75g/3oz butter or margarine

<u>For the filling:</u>
50g/2oz butter, softened to room temperature
115g/4oz icing sugar
75g/3oz ground almonds
Grated zest and juice of 1 lemon
Walnut halves and glacé cherries to decorate

Sift the flour and salt into a mixing bowl, and rub in the butter or margarine until the mixture resembles fine breadcrumbs. Use a round-bladed knife to stir in 2-3 tablespoonfuls of cold water, until the mixture can be gathered into a ball of dough. Knead the dough lightly until it is smooth and elastic, then wrap it in clingfilm and put it into the fridge to rest for 30 minutes.

Pre-heat the oven to 200°C/400°F/Gas Mark 6. Roll out the pastry on a lightly floured surface, and use it to line a greased flan tin. Prick the pastry all over with a fork to allow steam to escape during cooking. Put a piece of greaseproof paper on the pastry base and cover it with baking beans, then bake blind in the pre-heated oven for 10 minutes. Remove from the oven, and take out the paper and baking beans. Reduce the oven temperature to 180°C/350°F/Gas Mark 4.

Cream together the butter and icing sugar until the mixture is light and fluffy. Work in the ground almonds, the lemon zest and lemon juice. Spread the mixture evenly into the pastry case, then decorate the top with the walnut halves and glacé cherries. Bake in the oven at the reduced temperature for 25 minutes.

NELSON'S SLICES

This version of bread pudding is called Nelson's Slices, or Nelson's Cake, in Norfolk, after one of the county's most famous sons, Admiral Lord Nelson, who was born at Burnham Thorpe near King's Lynn in 1758. A statue of Lord Nelson stands in the cathedral close at Norwich, and he is also commemorated in Norfolk with a monument at South Denes, Great Yarmouth. This recipe is a good way of using up old bread past its best. The chopped peel can be substituted with an extra 50g/2oz of dried fruit if preferred.

> 8 thick slices of day-old white bread, including the crusts
> 300ml/ ½ pint milk
> 1 dessert apple
> 350g/12oz mixed dried fruit – currants, raisins, sultanas
> 50g/2oz chopped mixed peel (or extra dried fruit, if preferred)
> 115g/4oz soft, dark brown sugar
> 2 tablespoonfuls orange marmalade
> 50g/2oz self-raising flour
> 2 eggs, beaten
> 1 teaspoonful lemon juice
> 1 teaspoonful ground cinnamon
> 2 tablespoonfuls ground mixed spice
> 115g/4oz butter

Pre-heat the oven to 150°C/300°F/Gas Mark 2, and grease a baking or roasting tin about 28cms x 20cms (11 x 8 inches). Break the bread (including the crusts) into small pieces, place in a mixing bowl and add the milk. Leave the bread to soak for 30 minutes, then beat it well with a fork to break up any lumps and form a smooth mixture. Peel and core the apple, then grate it into the bread mixture. Add the dried fruit and peel, the sugar, marmalade, flour, beaten eggs, lemon juice, cinnamon and mixed spice, and mix it all together thoroughly. Melt the butter in a pan over a gentle heat, then pour half into the mixture, and beat it in well. Spread the mixture evenly into the prepared tin, then drizzle the remaining melted butter over the surface. Bake in the pre-heated oven for 2 hours. Increase the oven temperature to 180°C/350°F/Gas Mark 4, and bake for a further 30 minutes. Remove from the oven. This can be eaten hot as a pudding, with custard or cream. Alternatively, dredge the surface liberally with sugar, leave to cool and then cut into squares, to serve cold as a cake.

RECIPE

NORFOLK VINEGAR CAKE

This is an old Norfolk farmhouse recipe for a good, simple fruit cake. The recipe needs no eggs, and was probably made by the farmer's wife at the times when the hens were not laying.

> 225g/8oz butter
> 450g/1 lb plain flour
> 225g/8oz sugar
> 225g/8oz raisins
> 225g/8oz sultanas
> 250ml/8 fl oz milk
> 2 tablespoonfuls wine or cider vinegar
> 1 teaspoonful bicarbonate of soda,
>   mixed with 1 tablespoonful of milk

Pre-heat the oven to 180°C/350°F/Gas Mark 4.

Rub the butter into the flour to give a crumb-like consistency, then mix in the sugar and the fruit. Put the milk into a large jug or bowl and add the vinegar. Pour the bicarbonate of soda and milk mixture into the milk and vinegar – it will froth up and may overflow, so it is best to hold it over the mixing bowl while doing this.

Stir the liquid into the cake mixture, beat well and put it into a well-greased 23cm (9 inch) cake tin. Bake in the pre-heated oven for 30 minutes, then reduce the heat to 150°C/300°F/Gas Mark 2 and bake for a further 1¼ hours. Cover the top of the cake with foil if it starts to darken.

This cake will keep up to a week in an airtight container, and the flavour improves all the time.

WYMONDHAM, THE MARKET CROSS c1965 W159040

RECIPES

LAVENDER SCONES

In spring and summer, the fields of the Norfolk Lavender farm near Heacham are purple with fragrant flowers. Lavender is used in a wide variety of products, but can also be used in cooking. You can buy dried culinary lavender flowers from the Norfolk Lavender farm or online from its website (www.norfolk-lavender.co.uk), or use lavender grown in your own garden – use a variety of 'sweet' English lavender rather than the tufted French lavender variety ('Lavandula stoechas'), which has an unpleasant flavour and can be toxic. English lavender varieties 'Lavandula angustifolia' (sometimes called 'Lavandula officinalis') and 'Lavandula Munstead' give the best results for culinary purposes. Choose lavender sprigs that are deep purple and still in bud, before the flowers have opened. Lavender gives these scones a lovely fragrant flavour, and they are spectacular served with quince or crab apple jelly, if you can find or make some. This amount makes about 8-9 scones.

> 225g/8oz plain flour
> 1 teaspoonful bicarbonate of soda
> 2 teaspoonfuls cream of tartar
> 50g/2oz softened butter
> 25g/1oz caster sugar
> 2 teaspoonfuls fresh, or 1 teaspoonful dried, lavender florets
> 150ml/ ¼ pint semi-skimmed milk, warmed slightly

Pre-heat the oven to 200°C/400°F/Gas Mark 6, and grease a baking tray. Sieve the flour, bicarbonate of soda and cream of tartar into a mixing bowl. Rub in the butter, then stir in the sugar and lavender. Stir in the milk, using a round-bladed knife, to form a soft dough. Knead the dough gently for a few seconds, then lightly roll or pat it out on a floured surface to about 2cms (¾ inch) thick. Use a 6cms (2½ inch) fluted cutter to stamp out scone rounds, then re-roll the trimmings and cut out more. Place the rounds on the baking tray and bake in the pre-heated oven for 8-10 minutes, until they are well-risen and golden brown – do not overcook them, or their soft, light texture will be spoiled. Cool on a wire tray. These are lovely eaten whilst they are still warm, spread with butter, jam and clotted or very thick cream.

SPICED APPLE CAKE

Norfolk has been famous as an apple growing region for centuries, and there used to be extensive commercial orchards in south and east Norfolk, and towards the Fenland region. A number of apple varieties were developed in Norfolk, such as Norfolk Royal Russet, Lynn's Pippin, Norfolk Honey Russet, Norfolk Royal Red, Norfolk Summer Broad, Norfolk Green Queen, Striped Beefing and Norfolk Beauty. Cooking apples are traditionally used in this recipe for a spicy apple cake, but most dessert apples can also be used successfully if necessary.

> 225g/8oz self-raising flour
> 1 heaped teaspoonful baking powder
> 115g/4oz butter or margarine
> A pinch of salt
> 225g/8oz prepared weight of apples, peeled,
>   cored and chopped into small pieces
> 115g/4oz soft brown or caster sugar
> 1 egg
> 1 dessertspoonful milk
> 50g/2oz raisins and/or sultanas
> 1 teaspoonful ground cinnamon
> 1 teaspoonful ground mixed spice
> A little extra sugar to sprinkle on top

Pre-heat the oven to 190°C/375°F/Gas Mark 5 (slightly less for a fan oven) and grease and line a 20-22cm (8-9 inch) round cake tin. Sift the flour, baking powder and salt into a bowl. Rub in the butter or margarine until the mixture resembles breadcrumbs. Add the chopped apple pieces to the mixture, and then add the sugar and the dried fruit and spices. Beat the egg with the milk, and add to the mixture. Mix it all together well, to form a firm dough – it will seem quite stiff, but this is how it is meant to be, as the apples will cook down to form a moist cake. Turn the mixture into the prepared cake tin, smooth the top and sprinkle the top with sugar. Bake just below the centre of the pre-heated oven for about 45 minutes, until the top of the cake is golden brown and firm when you gently press down on it. Leave to cool in the tin for 15 minutes, then turn out the cake on to a wire rack. This can be eaten either hot as a delicious pudding, served with cream, custard or ice-cream, or cold as a cake. If eating as a cake, leave on the wire rack to cool completely, and store in an airtight tin.

RECIPE

YARMOUTH BISCUITS

350g/12oz plain flour
175g/6oz currants
225g/8oz butter, softened to room temperature
225g/8oz caster sugar
3 eggs, beaten

Pre-heat the oven to 190°C/375°F/Gas Mark 5 and grease two baking sheets. Mix together the currants, butter, sugar, flour and beaten eggs to make a thick paste. Roll out the dough and cut it into rounds. Place the rounds on the greased baking sheets and bake in the pre-heated oven for 15-20 minutes, until the biscuits are golden brown.

GREAT YARMOUTH, BRITANNIA PIER 1904 52337

RECIPE

NORFOLK FAIR BUTTONS

These small, crunchy biscuits, flavoured with lemon and ginger, were traditionally sold at fairs throughout the county in the past.

> 225g/8oz plain flour
> Half a teaspoonful ground ginger
> Half a teaspoonful bicarbonate of soda
> 50g/2oz butter, margarine or lard, cut into small pieces
> 115g/4oz soft dark brown sugar
> 2 tablespoonfuls golden syrup
> Grated rind of 1 lemon

Pre-heat the oven to 180°C/350°F/Gas Mark 4.

Sift together the flour, ground ginger, and bicarbonate of soda into a mixing bowl. Use your fingertips to rub in the butter, margarine or lard until the mixture resembles fine breadcrumbs. Add the sugar, grated lemon rind and the golden syrup and mix it all together thoroughly to form a firm dough (the golden syrup can be warmed slightly before being added, to make it easier to mix, if preferred). Roll out the dough on a lightly floured surface, and cut into small rounds about 5cm (2 inches) in diameter. Place the rounds onto greased baking sheets, spaced well apart, and bake in the pre-heated oven for about 10-12 minutes, until they are golden brown.

Carefully lift the biscuits off the sheets using a palette knife, and leave them to cool on wire rack. They will become crispy as they cool. Store in an airtight container.

DEREHAM, MARKET PLACE 1898 42757

FRANCIS FRITH

PIONEER VICTORIAN PHOTOGRAPHER

Francis Frith, founder of the world-famous photographic archive, was a complex and multi-talented man. A devout Quaker and a highly successful Victorian businessman, he was philosophical by nature and pioneering in outlook. By 1855 he had already established a wholesale grocery business in Liverpool, and sold it for the astonishing sum of £200,000, which is the equivalent today of over £15,000,000. Now in his thirties, and captivated by the new science of photography, Frith set out on a series of pioneering journeys up the Nile and to the Near East.

INTRIGUE AND EXPLORATION

He was the first photographer to venture beyond the sixth cataract of the Nile. Africa was still the mysterious 'Dark Continent', and Stanley and Livingstone's historic meeting was a decade into the future. The conditions for picture taking confound belief. He laboured for hours in his wicker dark-room in the sweltering heat of the desert, while the volatile chemicals fizzed dangerously in their trays. Back in London he exhibited his photographs and was 'rapturously cheered' by members of the Royal Society. His reputation as a photographer was made overnight.

VENTURE OF A LIFE-TIME

By the 1870s the railways had threaded their way across the country, and Bank Holidays and half-day Saturdays had been made obligatory by Act of Parliament. All of a sudden the working man and his family were able to enjoy days out, take holidays, and see a little more of the world.

With typical business acumen, Francis Frith foresaw that these new tourists would enjoy having souvenirs to commemorate their days out. For the next thirty years he travelled the country by train and by pony and trap, producing fine photographs of seaside resorts and beauty spots that were keenly bought by millions of Victorians. These prints were painstakingly pasted into family albums and pored over during the dark nights of winter, rekindling precious memories of summer excursions. Frith's studio was soon supplying retail shops all over the country, and by 1890 F Frith & Co had become the greatest specialist photographic publishing company in the world, with over 2,000 sales outlets, and pioneered the picture postcard.

FRANCIS FRITH'S LEGACY

Francis Frith had died in 1898 at his villa in Cannes, his great project still growing. By 1970 the archive he created contained over a third of a million pictures showing 7,000 British towns and villages.

Frith's legacy to us today is of immense significance and value, for the magnificent archive of evocative photographs he created provides a unique record of change in the cities, towns and villages throughout Britain over a century and more. Frith and his fellow studio photographers revisited locations many times down the years to update their views, compiling for us an enthralling and colourful pageant of British life and character.

We are fortunate that Frith was dedicated to recording the minutiae of everyday life. For it is this sheer wealth of visual data, the painstaking chronicle of changes in dress, transport, street layouts, buildings, housing and landscape that captivates us so much today, offering us a powerful link with the past and with the lives of our ancestors.

Computers have now made it possible for Frith's many thousands of images to be accessed almost instantly. The archive offers every one of us an opportunity to examine the places where we and our families have lived and worked down the years. Its images, depicting our shared past, are now bringing pleasure and enlightenment to millions around the world a century and more after his death.

For further information visit: www.francisfrith.com

INTERIOR DECORATION

Frith's photographs can be seen framed and as giant wall murals in thousands of pubs, restaurants, hotels, banks, retail stores and other public buildings throughout Britain. These provide interesting and attractive décor, generating strong local interest and acting as a powerful reminder of gentler days in our increasingly busy and frenetic world.

FRITH PRODUCTS

All Frith photographs are available as prints and posters in a variety of different sizes and styles. In the UK we also offer a range of other gift and stationery products illustrated with Frith photographs, although many of these are not available for delivery outside the UK – see our web site for more information on the products available for delivery in your country.

THE INTERNET

Over 100,000 photographs of Britain can be viewed and purchased on the Frith web site. The web site also includes memories and reminiscences contributed by our customers, who have personal knowledge of localities and of the people and properties depicted in Frith photographs. If you wish to learn more about a specific town or village you may find these reminiscences fascinating to browse. Why not add your own comments if you think they would be of interest to others? See **www.francisfrith.com**

PLEASE HELP US BRING FRITH'S PHOTOGRAPHS TO LIFE

Our authors do their best to recount the history of the places they write about. They give insights into how particular towns and villages developed, they describe the architecture of streets and buildings, and they discuss the lives of famous people who lived there. But however knowledgeable our authors are, the story they tell is necessarily incomplete.

Frith's photographs are so much more than plain historical documents. They are living proofs of the flow of human life down the generations. They show real people at real moments in history; and each of those people is the son or daughter of someone, the brother or sister, aunt or uncle, grandfather or grandmother of someone else. All of them lived, worked and played in the streets depicted in Frith's photographs.

We would be grateful if you would give us your insights into the places shown in our photographs: the streets and buildings, the shops, businesses and industries. Post your memories of life in those streets on the Frith website: what it was like growing up there, who ran the local shop and what shopping was like years ago; if your workplace is shown tell us about your working day and what the building is used for now. Read other visitors' memories and reconnect with your shared local history and heritage. With your help more and more Frith photographs can be brought to life, and vital memories preserved for posterity, and for the benefit of historians in the future.

Wherever possible, we will try to include some of your comments in future editions of our books. Moreover, if you spot errors in dates, titles or other facts, please let us know, because our archive records are not always completely accurate—they rely on 140 years of human endeavour and hand-compiled records. You can email us using the contact form on the website.

Thank you!

For further information, trade, or author enquiries
please contact us at the address below:

**The Francis Frith Collection, Oakley Business Park,
Wylye Road, Dinton, Wiltshire SP3 5EU England.**
Tel: +44 (0)1722 716 376 Fax: +44 (0)1722 716 881
e-mail: sales@francisfrith.co.uk **www.francisfrith.com**